A TASTE OF CHICKEN SOUP

FOR THE

COUPLE'S SOUL

A TASTE OF
CHICKEN SOUP

FOR THE

COUPLE'S SOUL

Inspirational Stories About
Love and Relationships

Jack Canfield, Mark Victor Hansen
Barbara De Angelis, Ph.D.,
Mark Donnely, Chrissy Donnelly

Health Communications, Inc.
Deerfield Beach, Florida

www.hcibooks.com
www.chickensoup.com

Thinking of You. Reprinted by permission of Alicia von Stamwitz. ©1998 Alicia von Stamwitz.

Someone to Watch Over Me. Reprinted by permission of Sharon M. Wajda. ©1998 Sharon M. Wajda.

The Fortune Cookie Prophecy. Reprinted by permission of Don Buehner. ©1998 Don Buehner.

The Promise. Reprinted by permission of Thomas F. Crum. ©1998 Thomas F. Crum.

Love Me Tender. Reprinted by permission of Jacklyn Lee Lindstrom. ©1998 Jacklyn Lee Lindstrom.

A Legend of Love. Reprinted by permission of LeAnn Thieman. ©1998 LeAnn Thieman.

Baby, You Are . . . Reprinted by permission of David L. Weatherford. ©1998 David L. Weatherford.

A Sign of His Love. Reprinted by permission of Patricia Forbes. ©1998 Patricia Forbes.

One Last Good-Bye. Reprinted by permission of Karen Corkern Babb. ©1998 Karen Corkern Babb.

Belonging. Reprinted by permission of Bob Welch. ©1998 Bob Welch.

Library of Congress Cataloging-in-Publication Data is on file with the Library of Congress

©2006 Jack Canfield, Mark Victor Hansen, Barbara De Angelis, Mark Donnelly and Chrissy Donnelly

ISBN 0-75730-508-3

HCI, its Logos and Marks are trademarks of Health Communications, Inc.

Publisher: Health Communications, Inc.
      3201 S.W. 15th Street
      Deerfield Beach, FL 33442-8190

"We are each of us angels
with only one wing. And we can fly
only by embracing each other."

Luciano de Crescenzo

From our hearts to yours,
we dedicate this book to everyone
who has ever been in love, or
hopes to be in love again.

Contents

Introduction

Love is the most powerful, magical force in the universe, and there is nowhere it displays its beauty and wonder more than in the intimate relationship between two people. We wrote *Chicken Soup for the Couple's Soul* hoping to capture that mystery and wonder in words. This "taste"ful excerpt from that book is for husbands and wives and lovers and anyone who dreams of finding their soul's true mate.

Some loves endure a lifetime; others are destined to last only a while. But no matter what the outcome, when love enters our lives, it never leaves without transforming us at the very depth of our being.

Like love itself, the stories in this book reflect every season, mood and color of emotion: sweet beginnings; challenging and deepening intimacy; grief at good-byes;

astonishment when we rediscover lost love.

Some stories will make you laugh. Some will make you cry. But above all, these stories pay tribute to love's ability to endure, beyond years, beyond difficulty, beyond distance, beyond even death.

There is no miracle greater than love. It is God's most precious gift to us. We offer this book as our gift to you. May it open your heart, uplift your mind, inspire your spirit, and be a sweet companion on your own heart's journey. And may your life always be blessed with love.

Thinking of You

*To live in hearts we leave behind
is not to die.*

THOMAS CAMPBELL

Sophie's face faded into the gray winter light of the sitting room. She dozed in the armchair that Joe had bought for her on their fortieth anniversary. The room was warm and quiet. Outside it was snowing lightly.

At a quarter past one the mailman turned the corner onto Allen Street. He was behind on his route, not because of the snow, but because it was Valentine's

Day and there was more mail than usual. He passed Sophie's house without looking up. Twenty minutes later he climbed back into his truck and drove off.

Sophie stirred when she heard the mail truck pull away, then took off her glasses and wiped her mouth and eyes with the handkerchief she always carried in her sleeve. She pushed herself up using the arm of the chair for support, straightened slowly and smoothed the lap of her dark green housedress.

Her slippers made a soft, shuffling sound on the bare floor as she walked to the kitchen. She stopped at the sink to wash the two dishes she had left on the counter after lunch. Then she filled a plastic cup halfway with water and took her pills. It was one forty-five.

There was a rocker in the sitting room by the front window. Sophie eased herself into it. In a half-hour the children would be passing by on their way home from school. Sophie waited, rocking and watching the snow.

The boys came first, as always, running and calling out things Sophie could not hear. Today they were making snowballs as they went, throwing them at one another. One snowball missed and smacked hard into Sophie's window. She jerked backward, and the rocker slipped off the edge of her oval rag rug.

The girls dilly-dallied after the boys, in twos and threes, cupping their mittened hands over their mouths and giggling. Sophie wondered if they were telling each other about the valentines they had received at school. One pretty girl with long brown hair stopped and pointed to the window where Sophie sat watching. Sophie slipped her face behind the drapes, suddenly self-conscious.

When she looked out again, the boys and girls were gone. It was cold by the window, but she stayed there watching the snow cover the children's footprints.

A florist's truck turned onto Allen Street. Sophie followed it with her eyes. It was moving slowly. Twice it stopped and started again. Then the driver pulled up in front of Mrs. Mason's house next door and parked.

Who would be sending Mrs. Mason flowers? Sophie wondered. *Her daughter in Wisconsin? Or her brother? No, her brother was very ill. It was probably her daughter. How nice of her.*

Flowers made Sophie think of Joe and, for a moment, she let the aching memory fill her. Tomorrow was the fifteenth. Eight months since his death.

The flower man was knocking at Mrs. Mason's front door. He carried a long white and green box and a clipboard. No one seemed to be answering. Of course! It was Friday—Mrs. Mason quilted at the church on Friday afternoons. The delivery man looked around, then started toward Sophie's house.

Sophie shoved herself out of the rocker and stood close to the drapes. The man knocked. Her hands trembled as she straightened her hair. She reached her front hall on his third knock.

"Yes?" she said, peering around a slightly opened door.

"Good afternoon, ma'am," the man said loudly. "Would you take a delivery for your neighbor?"

"Yes," Sophie answered, pulling the door wide open.

"Where would you like me to put them?" the man asked politely as he strode in.

"In the kitchen, please. On the table." The man looked big to Sophie. She could hardly see his face between his green cap and full beard. Sophie was glad he left quickly, and she locked the door after him.

The box was as long as the kitchen table. Sophie drew near to it and bent over to read the lettering: "Natalie's Flowers for

Every Occasion." The rich smell of roses engulfed her. She closed her eyes and took slower breaths, imagining yellow roses. Joe had always chosen yellow. "To my sunshine," he would say, presenting the extravagant bouquet. He would laugh delightedly, kiss her on the forehead, then take her hands in his and sing to her "You Are My Sunshine."

It was five o'clock when Mrs. Mason knocked at Sophie's front door. Sophie was still at the kitchen table. The flower box was now open though, and she held the roses on her lap, swaying slightly and stroking the delicate yellow petals. Mrs. Mason knocked again, but Sophie did not hear her, and after several minutes the neighbor left.

Sophie rose a little while later, laying the flowers on the kitchen table. Her cheeks were flushed. She dragged a stepstool across the kitchen floor and lifted a white porcelain vase from the top corner cabinet.

Using a drinking glass, she filled the vase with water, then tenderly arranged the roses and greens, and carried them into the sitting room.

She was smiling as she reached the middle of the room. She turned slightly and began to dip and twirl in small slow circles. She stepped lightly, gracefully, around the sitting room, into the kitchen, down the hall, back again. She danced till her knees grew weak, and then she dropped into the armchair and slept.

At a quarter past six, Sophie awoke with a start. Someone was knocking on the back door this time. It was Mrs. Mason.

"Hello, Sophie," Mrs. Mason said. "How are you? I knocked at five and was a little worried when you didn't come. Were you napping?" She chattered as she wiped her snowy boots on the welcome mat and stepped inside. "I just hate the snow, don't you? The radio says we might have six inches by midnight, but you can never trust them, you know. Do you remember last winter when they predicted four inches and we had twenty-one? Twenty-one! And they said we'd have a mild winter this year. Ha! I don't think it's been over zero in weeks. Do you know my oil bill was $263 last month? For my little house!"

Sophie was only half-listening. She had remembered the roses suddenly and was turning hot with shame. The empty flower box was behind her on the kitchen table. What would she say to Mrs. Mason?

"I don't know how much longer I can keep paying the bills. If only Alfred, God bless him, had been as careful with money as your Joseph. Joseph! Oh, good heavens! I almost forgot about the roses."

Sophie's cheeks burned. She began to stammer an apology, stepping aside to reveal the empty box.

"Oh, good," Mrs. Mason interrupted. "You put the roses in water. Then you saw the card. I hope it didn't startle you to see Joseph's handwriting. Joseph had asked me to bring you the roses the first year, so I could explain for him. He didn't want to alarm you. His 'Rose Trust,' I think he called it. He arranged it with the florist last April. Such a good man, your Joseph. . . ."

But Sophie had stopped listening. Her heart was pounding as she picked up the small white envelope she had missed earlier. It had been lying beside the flower box all the time. With trembling hands, she removed the card.

"To my sunshine," it said. "I love you with all my heart. Try to be happy when you think of me. Love, Joe."

Alicia von Stamwitz

Someone to Watch Over Me

The passengers on the bus watched sympathetically as the attractive young woman with the white cane made her way carefully up the steps. She paid the driver and, using her hands to feel the location of the seats, walked down the aisle and found the seat he'd told her was empty. Then she settled in, placed her briefcase on her lap and rested her cane against her leg.

It had been a year since Susan, thirty-four, became blind. Due to a medical misdiagnosis she had been rendered sightless, and she was suddenly thrown into a world of darkness, anger, frustration and self-pity. Once a fiercely independent woman, Susan now felt condemned by this terrible twist of fate to become a powerless, helpless burden on everyone around her. "How could this have happened to me?" she would plead, her heart knotted with anger. But no matter how much she cried or ranted or prayed, she knew the painful truth—her sight was never going to return.

A cloud of depression hung over Susan's once optimistic spirit. Just getting through each day was an exercise in frustration and exhaustion. And all she had to cling to was her husband Mark.

Mark was an Air Force officer and he loved Susan with all of his heart. When she first lost her sight, he watched her sink into despair and was determined to help his wife gain the strength and confidence she needed to become independent again. Mark's military background had trained him well to deal with sensitive situations, and yet he knew this was the most difficult battle he would ever face.

Finally, Susan felt ready to return to her job, but how would she get there? She used to take the bus, but was now too frightened to get around the city by herself. Mark volunteered to drive her to work each day, even though they worked at opposite ends of the city. At first, this comforted Susan and fulfilled Mark's need to protect his sightless wife who was so insecure about performing the slightest task. Soon, however, Mark realized that this arrangement wasn't working—it was hectic, and costly. *Susan is going to have to start taking the bus again,* he admitted to himself. But just the thought of mentioning it to her made him cringe. She was still so fragile, so angry. How would she react?

Just as Mark predicted, Susan was horrified at the idea of taking the bus again. "I'm blind!" she responded bitterly. "How am I supposed to know where I'm going? I feel like you're abandoning me."

Mark's heart broke to hear these words, but he knew what had to be done. He promised Susan that each morning and evening he would ride the bus with her, for as long as it took, until she got the hang of it.

And that is exactly what happened. For two solid weeks, Mark, military uniform and all, accompanied Susan to and from work each day. He taught her how to rely on her other senses, specifically her hearing, to determine where she was and how to adapt to her new environment. He helped her befriend the bus drivers who could watch out for her, and save her a seat. He made her laugh, even on those not-so-good days when she would trip exiting the bus, or drop her briefcase full of papers on the aisle floor.

Each morning they made the journey together, and Mark would take a cab back to his office. Although this routine was even more costly and exhausting than the previous one, Mark knew it was only a matter of time before Susan would be able to ride the bus on her own. He believed in her, in the Susan he used to know before she'd lost her sight, who wasn't afraid of any challenge and who would never, ever quit.

Finally, Susan decided that she was ready to try the trip on her own. Monday morning arrived, and before she left, she threw her arms around Mark, her temporary bus riding companion, her husband, and her best friend. Her eyes filled with tears of gratitude for his loyalty, his patience, and his love. She said good-bye, and for the first time, they went their separate ways.

Monday, Tuesday, Wednesday, Thursday. . . . Each day on her own went perfectly, and Susan had never felt better. She was doing it! She was going to work all by herself.

On Friday morning, Susan took the bus to work as usual. As she was paying her fare to exit the bus, the driver said, "Boy, I sure envy you."

Susan wasn't sure if the driver was speaking to her or not. After all, who on earth would ever envy a blind woman who had struggled just to find the courage to live for the past year? Curious, she asked the driver, "Why do you say that you envy me?"

The driver responded, "It must feel so good to be taken care of and protected like you are."

Susan had no idea what the driver was talking about, and again asked, "What do you mean?"

The driver answered, "You know, every morning for the past week, a fine looking gentleman in a military uniform has been standing across the corner watching you when you get off the bus. He makes sure you cross the street safely and he watches until you enter your office building. Then he blows you a kiss, gives you a little salute and walks away. You are one lucky lady."

Tears of happiness poured down Susan's cheeks. For although she couldn't physically see him, she had always felt Mark's presence. She was lucky, so lucky, for he had given her a gift more powerful than sight, a gift she didn't need to see to believe—the gift of love that can bring light where there had been darkness.

Sharon Wajda

The Fortune Cookie Prophecy

There is no surprise more magical than the surprise of being loved; it is God's finger on man's shoulder.

CHARLES MORGAN

I was married three times before I was seven years old.

My older brother Gary performed the ceremonies in our basement. Gary was good at entertaining the family and neighborhood kids with his creative ideas. Since I was the youngest boy in our group, I was often on the receiving end of his creativity.

What I remember most about those

weddings is that all the girls were at least five years older than I was, and they all had beautiful eyes that sparkled when they laughed. Those weddings taught me to imagine what it would be like to find my soul mate one day and to be sure that I would know her by her beautiful eyes.

Puberty hit me late. I was still afraid of the opposite sex when I was fifteen, and yet I prayed every night for the girl I would marry. I asked God to help her do well in school and to be happy and full of energy—wherever and whoever she was.

I first kissed a girl when I was twenty-one. From that time forward, I dated many beautiful and talented young ladies, searching for the girl I had prayed for in my youth and still certain that I would know her by her eyes.

One day, my phone rang. "Don," it was my mother. "You know I told you about the Addisons, who moved in next door to us. Well, Clara Addison keeps asking me to invite you over for cards some night."

"Sorry, Mom, I've got a date that night."

"How could you? I haven't even told you what night it is?" my mother responded with exasperation.

"It doesn't matter when. I'm sure the Addisons are nice people, but I'm not going to waste an evening socializing with people who don't have any eligible daughters."

That's how stubborn I was—I was positive that there was no reason for me to go to visit the Addisons.

Years passed. I was twenty-six, and my friends were getting nervous about my prospects. They kept lining up blind dates for me. Many of these dates were fiascoes, and they were interfering with my social life. So I made up a few rules about blind dates:

1. No dates recommended by my mother

(moms don't understand the sex-appeal factor).

2. No dates recommended by a female (they're too easy on each other).

3. No dates recommended by a single guy friend (if she's so awesome, how come he hasn't asked her out?).

In three simple steps, I eliminated 90 percent of all my blind dates, including one recommended by my old friend Karen. She called one evening to tell me that she had become good friends with a beautiful girl who reminded her of me. She said she knew we would hit it off.

"Sorry," I said, "you're ruled out by rule number two."

"Don," she said, "you're crazy, and your silly rules are eliminating the girl you've been waiting for. But have it your way. Just take her name and phone number, and when you change your mind, call her."

To get Karen to stop bothering me about

it, I said I would. The girl's name was Susan Maready. I never called her.

Just a couple of weeks later, I ran into my old buddy Ted in the university cafeteria. "Ted," I said. "You look like you're walking on air."

"Can you see stars under my feet?" he said, laughing. "The fact is, I just got engaged last night."

"Hey, congratulations!"

"Yeah," he said, "at thirty-two, I was beginning to wonder if any woman was going to have me." He pulled his wallet out of his pocket. "Here," he said, suddenly serious, "look at this."

It was a thin strip of paper from a fortune cookie. "You will be married within a year," it said.

"That's wild," I said. "They usually say something that would fit anyone, like 'You have a magnetic personality.' They were really taking a chance with that one."

"No kidding," he said. "And look at me now."

A few weeks later, my roommate Charlie and I were eating dinner at a Chinese restaurant. I shared this story about Ted's fortune cookie prediction, and his subsequent engagement. Just then, the waiter brought over our post-meal fortune cookies. Charlie laughed at the coincidence as we opened our cookies. Mine said, "You have a magnetic personality." His said, "You or a close friend will be married within a year." A chill ran up my spine. This was really strange. Something told me to ask Charlie if I could keep his fortune, and he handed it to me with a smile.

Not long afterward, my classmate Brian said he wanted to introduce me to a young woman named Susan Maready. I was sure I'd heard that name before, but couldn't remember how or where. Since Brian was married, and therefore I wouldn't be breaking my "rules" about being fixed up by single guys, I accepted his offer to meet Susan.

Susan and I spoke on the phone, and planned a bike ride and a cookout. Then, the meeting—and as soon as I saw her, my heart started beating hard and wouldn't stop. Her large green eyes did something to me I couldn't explain. But somewhere in me, I knew that it was love at first sight.

After that wonderful evening, I remembered that this hadn't been the first time someone tried to fix me up with Susan. It all came back to me. Her name had been popping up all over the place for a long time. So the next time I had a chance to talk to Brian alone, I asked him about it.

He squirmed and tried to change the subject.

"What is it, Brian?" I asked.

"You'll have to ask Susan," was all he'd say.

So I did.

"I was going to tell you," she said. "I was going to tell you."

"Come on, Susan," I said. "Tell me what? I can't stand the suspense."

"I've been in love with you for years," she said, "since the first time I saw you from the Addisons' living room window. Yes—it was me they wanted you to meet. But you wouldn't let anyone introduce us. You wouldn't let the Addisons set us up; you wouldn't take Karen's word for it that we would like each other. I thought I was never going to meet you."

My heart swelled with love, and I laughed at myself. "Karen was right," I said. "My rules were crazy."

"You're not mad?" she asked.

"Are you kidding?" I said. "I'm impressed. I've got only one rule for blind dating now."

She gave me a strange look. "What's that?"

"Never again," I said and kissed her.

We were married seven months later.

Susan and I are convinced that we are true soul mates. When I was fifteen and praying for my future wife, she was fourteen and praying for her future husband.

After we had been married a couple of months, Susan said to me, "Do you want to hear something really strange?"

"Sure," I said. "I love to hear strange things."

"Well, about ten months ago, before I'd met you, my friends and I were at this Chinese restaurant, and . . ." She pulled a slip of paper from a fortune cookie out of her wallet:

"You will be married within a year. . . ."

Don Buehner

The Promise

My lifetime listens to yours.
MURIEL RUCKEYSER

One evening I found myself at a conference in Washington, D.C. And as fate would have it, Bucky Fuller happened to be making a presentation that evening at another conference in the very same hotel. I got to the ballroom in time to hear the end of Bucky's lecture. I was in awe of this little man in his eighties, with his clear mind, deep wisdom and boundless energy. At the end of the talk, we walked together through the underground parking lot to his airport limousine.

"I've got to go to New York City tonight for another presentation," he said, looking at me with an anxiousness that I had rarely seen in Bucky.

"You know, Annie's not doing well. I'm very concerned about her."

We hugged.

Bucky Fuller had once confided to me that he had promised his wife Annie to die before she did, so that he could be there to welcome her when it was her turn. I took the comment as a hope, not a commitment. Which shows how greatly I underestimated Buckminster Fuller.

Shortly after Bucky's presentation in New York, he learned that Annie had lapsed into a coma in a hospital in Los Angeles. Doctors felt that there was a good chance she would not regain consciousness. Bucky took the first flight he could get. Upon arriving in Los Angeles, he went immediately to Annie's bedside. Sitting beside her, he closed his eyes.

And quietly died.

The power to choose life fully was something that Bucky exemplified. So much so that he had the power to choose death when it was time, peacefully, with arms wide open to the universe that he served. It was simply another courageous step forward.

Hours later, Annie peacefully joined him in death. He had kept his promise. He was waiting for her.

Thomas F. Crum

Fifty Ways to Love Your Partner

1. Love yourself first.
2. Start each day with a hug.
3. Serve breakfast in bed.
4. Say "I love you" every time you part ways.
5. Compliment freely and often.
6. Appreciate—and   celebrate—your differences.
7. Live each day as if it's your last.
8. Write unexpected love letters.
9. Plant a seed together and nurture it to maturity.
10. Go on a date once every week.

11. Send flowers for no reason.
12. Accept and love each others' family and friends.
13. Make little signs that say "I love you" and post them all over the house.
14. Stop and smell the roses.
15. Kiss unexpectedly.
16. Seek out beautiful sunsets together.
17. Apologize sincerely.
18. Be forgiving.
19. Remember the day you fell in love— and recreate it.
20. Hold hands.
21. Say "I love you" with your eyes.
22. Let her cry in your arms.
23. Tell him you understand.
24. Drink toasts of love and commitment.
25. Do something arousing.
26. Let her give you directions when you're lost.
27. Laugh at his jokes.
28. Appreciate her inner beauty.

29. Do the other person's chores for a day.
30. Encourage wonderful dreams.
31. Commit a public display of affection.
32. Give loving massages with no strings attached.
33. Start a love journal and record your special moments.
34. Calm each others' fears.
35. Walk barefoot on the beach together.
36. Ask her to marry you again.
37. Say yes.
38. Respect each other.
39. Be your partner's biggest fan.
40. Give the love your partner wants to receive.
41. Give the love you want to receive.
42. Show interest in the other's work.
43. Work on a project together.
44. Build a fort with blankets.
45. Swing as high as you can on a swing set by moonlight.
46. Have a picnic indoors on a rainy day.

47. Never go to bed mad.
48. Put your partner first in your prayers.
49. Kiss each other goodnight.
50. Sleep like spoons.

Mark and Chrissy Donnelly

Love Me Tender

*The most difficult year of marriage
is the one you're in.*

Franklin P. Jones

*It's raining. Of course. Why would it do any-
thing else on the worst day of my life?*

Eighteen-year-old Libby Dalton stared
out the window, her elbows propped on
the table, her chin buried in her fists.
Stacks of boxes cast sporadic ghostly pat-
terns on the wall as the lighting flickered
through the rain beating incessantly on
the windowpanes.

Within the hour, they'd be leaving home

and family to live in some godforsaken place called Levittown, New York.

Was it only a month ago that Johnny burst into the apartment with his great news . . . the job offer, the chance to get out of Milford and into something he really wanted? How could she tell him she could not leave her family—her home—her life?

Elizabeth Jane Berens and John Dalton Jr., the blond, blue-eyed cheerleader and the handsome football player, had been sweethearts all through high school: elected homecoming royalty their senior year and labeled in the yearbook as Milford High School's Cutest Couple.

It was the fifties, and life was sweet in small-town America. Elvis Presley was king, and his latest hit, "Love Me Tender," had just hit the airwaves. At the senior prom, Milford's cutest couple slow danced, lost in each other's arms as the band played "their song." Johnny's soft voice crooned the lyrics in her ear, and Libby's heart melted.

"Be careful," her mother warned. "You know what happens to girls who don't behave themselves."

Libby had no intention of being one of the girls talked about in the locker rooms. They would wait.

But on graduation night, without a word to anyone, they ran across the state line and stood before a justice of the peace. They could wait no longer.

On the arm of her new husband, Libby proudly displayed her wedding ring to dismayed parents who saw their dreams— the football scholarship, the college diploma, the long, white dress and veil, vanish like bubbles in the air.

"Are you pregnant?" her mother asked when she got Libby off to one side.

"No," Libby assured her, hurt at the suggestion.

It was fun at first, playing house in the tiny apartment where they never seemed to get enough of each other. Johnny worked full-time as a mechanic at Buckner's garage and attended vo-tech at night, training to be an electrician. Libby waited tables at the local diner. The newness soon wore off, and as they stumbled over each other in the close confines of two rooms, they dreamed and saved for a house of their own.

Now, a year later, Libby was five months pregnant, sick every day and had to give up her job. High school friends quit calling the couple, who no longer had money for dancing and movies. Frequent arguments replaced words of love, as hopes and plans for the future dissolved into the empty frustration of barely getting by. Libby spent her days, and lately her nights, alone in the tiny apartment, suspecting that Johnny might be "fooling around." Nobody works *every* night.

As she returned from another bout of morning sickness, Libby glanced in the mirror at the swollen body and unkempt hair.

Who could blame Johnny for looking around? What is there for him here? A baby coming, a fat, ugly wife and never any money.

Her mother fussed about the pale face and circles under her eyes. "You must take care of yourself, Libby," her mother told her. "Think of your husband, think of the baby."

That's all Libby did think about—the baby . . . that impersonal lump inside, ruining her figure and making her constantly sick.

Then came the day Johnny told her about the new job in Levittown.

"We'll be moving into a company house," he said, his eyes shining. "It's small, but it's better than this dump."

She nodded and blinked rapidly so he wouldn't see the tears. She couldn't leave Milford.

No one would be coming to say good-bye today. . . . It had been done last night at the farewell party. As Johnny hauled out the last box, she took a final walk through their first home, her footsteps echoing on bare wooden floors. The odor of furniture polish and wax still hung in the air. Faint voices filled the rooms as she remembered the night they waxed those floors, giggling and pushing each other, pausing in the middle to love each other. Two cluttered rooms, now cold and empty. Funny how quickly they became impersonal cubes as though no one had ever lived, or loved, there. She closed the door behind her for the last time and hurried out to the truck.

The weather worsened as they drove, along with her mood.

"It's a big company," Johnny said. "Levitton Manufacturing . . . electronic parts . . . a chance to get ahead. . . ."

She nodded briefly, then returned to staring out the window. He finally gave up his attempts at small talk, and they drove on in silence, broken only by the squeaky thumps of windshield wipers.

As they reached the outskirts of Levittown, the rain stopped and the sun shone through broken patches in the clouds.

"A good sign," Johnny said, looking up at the sky.

She nodded silently.

After a few wrong turns, they found their new home, and Libby stared solemnly at the tiny box in the middle of identical boxes, like Monopoly houses lined up on Oriental Avenue.

"Are you ever going to smile again, Lib?"

She climbed out of the cab and scolded herself. *Grow up, Libby. Do you think this is any easier for him?*

She wanted to say she was sorry, but the ever ready tears welled up and she turned away. Without a word, they carried boxes into the house, setting them down wherever they could find room.

"Sit down and rest, Lib," Johnny said. "I'll finish unloading."

She sat on a box and stared out the window. *At least it stopped raining.*

A knock interrupted her thoughts, and she opened the door to a girl about her own age, obviously pregnant, holding a small plate of cookies. "Welcome to the neighborhood," she said. "I'm Susan, but everybody calls me Souie."

They sat on boxes, eating cookies and comparing pregnancies, morning sickness and backaches. Souie was due in two months. Libby in four.

"I can come over tomorrow and help you settle in if you like," Souie said. "It's so good to have someone to talk to."

Amen, thought Libby.

After Souie left, Libby glanced around the room with a new eye. *Maybe some blue curtains in the kitchen. . . .*

The door suddenly sprang open and Johnny ran in, hurriedly digging through the boxes. He pulled out a small radio, plugged it into the wall socket, and suddenly "their song" and the voice of Elvis singing drifted into the kitchen.

They heard the disc jockey's voice over the music, ". . . and this request comes from a pair of newcomers in town. Congratulations to John and Libby Dalton on their wedding anniversary."

Johnny had remembered their anniversary. She had forgotten. Tears streamed down her face, and the wall of silence and self-pity she had built around herself crumbled.

He pulled her up to him, and she heard his voice singing soft and sweet in her ear.

Together they danced in between the packing cartons, clinging to each other as if discovering love for the first time. Sunlight filtered through the window in the new house in the new town, and as she felt the first kicks of the new life inside her, Libby Dalton learned the meaning of love.

Jacklyn Lee Lindstrom

A Legend of Love

*If love does not know how to give and take
without restrictions, it is not love,
but a transaction.*

EMMA GOLDMAN

Edward Wellman bade good-bye to his
family in the old country headed for a better life in America. Papa handed him the
family's savings hidden in a leather
satchel. "Times are desperate here," he
said, hugging his son goodbye. "You are
our hope." Edward boarded the Atlantic
freighter offering free transport to young
men willing to shovel coal in return for the

month-long journey. If Edward struck gold in the Colorado Rockies, the rest of the family could eventually join him.

For months, Edward worked his claim tirelessly, and the small vein of gold provided a moderate but steady income. At the end of each day, as he walked through the door of his two-room cabin, he yearned for the woman he loved to greet him. Leaving Ingrid behind before he could officially court her had been his only regret in accepting this American adventure. Their families had been friends for years and for as long as he could remember, he had secretly hoped to make Ingrid his wife. Her long, flowing hair and radiant smile made her the most beautiful of the Henderson sisters. He had just begun sitting by her at church picnics and making up silly reasons to stop by her house, just so he could see her. As he went to sleep in his cabin each night, Edward longed to stroke her auburn hair and hold her in his arms. Finally, he wrote to Papa, asking him to help make this dream come true.

After nearly a year, a telegraph came with a plan to make his life complete. Mr. Henderson had agreed to send his daughter to Edward in America. Because she was a hardworking young woman with a good mind for business, she would work alongside Edward for a year to help the mining business grow. By then both families could afford to come to America for their wedding.

Edward's heart soared with joy as he spent the next month trying to make the cabin into a home. He bought a cot for him to sleep on in the living area and tried to make his former bedroom suitable for a woman. Floral cloth from flour sacks replaced the burlap-bag curtains covering the grimy window. He arranged dried sage from the meadow into a tin-can vase on the nightstand.

At last, the day he had been waiting for his whole life arrived. With a bouquet of fresh-picked daisies in hand, he left for the train depot. Steam billowed and wheels screeched as the train crawled to a stop. Edward scanned every window looking for Ingrid's glowing hair and smile.

His heart beat with eager anticipation, then stopped with a sinking thud. Not Ingrid, but her older sister Marta, stepped down from the train. She stood shyly before him, her eyes cast down.

Edward only stared—dumbfounded. Then with shaking hands he offered Marta the bouquet. "Welcome," he whispered, his eyes burning. A smile etched across her plain face.

"I was pleased when Papa said you sent for me," Marta said, looking into his eyes briefly, before dropping her head again.

"I'll get your bags," Edward said with a fake smile. Together they headed for the buggy.

Mr. Henderson and Papa were right. Marta did have a great grasp of business.

While Edward worked the mine, she worked the office. From her makeshift desk in one corner of the living area, she kept detailed records of all claim activity. Within six months, their assets doubled.

Her delicious meals and quiet smile graced the cabin with a wonderful woman's touch. *But the wrong woman,* Edward mourned as he collapsed onto his cot each night. *Why did they send Marta?* Would he ever see Ingrid again? Was his lifelong dream to have her as his wife forsaken?

For a year, Marta and Edward worked and played and laughed, but never loved. Once, Marta had kissed Edward on the cheek before retiring to her room. He only smiled awkwardly. From then on, she seemed content with their exhilarating hikes in the mountains and long talks on the porch after suppers.

One spring afternoon, torrential rains washed down the hillside, eroding the entrance to their mine. Furiously, Edward filled sandbags and stacked them in the water's path. Soaked and exhausted, his frantic efforts seemed futile. Suddenly there was Marta at his side holding the next burlap bag open. Edward shoveled sand inside, then with the strength of any man, Marta hurled it onto the pile and opened another bag. For hours they worked, knee-deep in mud, until the rains diminished. Hand in hand, they walked back to the cabin. Over warm soup Edward sighed, "I never could have saved the mine without you. Thank you, Marta."

"You're welcome," she answered with her usual smile, then went quietly to her room.

A few days later, a telegraph came announcing the arrival of the Henderson and Wellman families next week. As much as he tried to stifle it, the thought of seeing Ingrid again started Edward's heart beating in the old familiar way.

Together, he and Marta went to the train station. They watched as their families exited the train at the far end of the platform. When Ingrid appeared, Marta turned to Edward. "Go to her," she said.

Astonished, Edward stammered, "What do you mean?"

"Edward, I have always known I was not the Henderson girl you intended to send for. I had watched you flirt with Ingrid at the church picnics." She nodded toward her sister descending the train steps. "I know it is she, not me, you desire for your wife."

"But . . ."

Marta placed her fingers over his lips. "Shhh," she hushed him. "I do love you, Edward. I always have. And because of that, all I really want is your happiness. Go to her."

He took her hand from his face and held it. As she gazed up at him, he saw for the first time how very beautiful she was. He recalled their walks in the meadows, their quiet evenings before the fire, her working beside him with the sandbags. It was then he realized what he had known for months.

"No, Marta. It is you I want." Sweeping her into his arms, he kissed her with all the love bursting inside him. Their families gathered around them chorusing, "We are here for the wedding!"

LeAnn Thieman

Baby, You Are . . .

my sunny sky,
my favorite high,
my bed so warm,
my port in a storm,
my sweetest gift,
my emotional lift,
my best friend
until the end,
my inspiration,
my destination,
my shining light,
my day and night,
my heart healer,
my anger chiller,
my pain reliever,
my spring fever,

my gem so rare,
my answered prayer,
my heart and soul,
my life made whole,
my merry-go-'round,
my "up" when I'm down,
my best chance,
my last dance,
my best shot,
my sweet kumquat,
my energizer,
my appetizer,
my morning sun,
my evening fun,
my dancing partner,
my heart's gardener,
my source of laughter,
my everafter,
my heaven sent,
for who I'm meant,
my burning fire,
my greatest desire,
my soul mate,
my sweet fate,
my dream lover,
my "before all others,"
my confidence,

my common sense,
my reason why
until I die.

Just in case you didn't know.

David L. Weatherford

A Sign of His Love

It never occurred to me that our airline tickets were to be round-trip for me and one-way for Don. We were on our way to Houston for open heart surgery, Don's third operation. But he was otherwise healthy and robust, and only sixty-one years old. His doctor felt confident that he would come through this valve replacement just fine. Others had survived two or more heart operations. Don would, too.

The day of the operation came. A very long day. Six hours into the procedure, the doctor came out to tell me that they could not get Don off the heart-lung machine. His heart would not kick back in. A left-ventricle assist was put in. After two days with this implanted machine, it had to be removed. He remained in a coma for five days on every conceivable life support. The morning that the doctors shook their heads and said it looked like we were losing the battle, I went in at the usual time, held his hand and told him how much I loved him, that I knew he was struggling to come back, but I needed to release him to do whatever he needed to do. "I'll always love you," I said. "I want you to know that if you have to go, I'll be all right." That night he died.

Back home to Denver—my loving brother accompanied me. My children came for the funeral, offering wonderful, loving support. Still, I was totally lost. I had found Don again, after parting from him in college thirty years ago, each of us leading our own lives, me in Houston, Don in Denver. I was divorced, and running across a letter and picture of this college sweetheart, I felt compelled to write him. A "hello across thirty years." I found his name in the Denver phone book and sent the letter. And I held my breath. He replied, and he told me his wife had just died two months prior to my letter. We corresponded and finally decided to meet again. What a reunion. We fell into the same easy, comfortable love we had known so many years ago. We married in April, two years after meeting again. I moved to Denver. We had six gentle, wonderful years together. We had planned on many, many more.

It was the day before the funeral and I was sitting out on my back patio, feeling like my life had ended too. More than anything, I wanted assurance that Don was okay now, that he was out of pain, at peace and that his spirit would always be near at hand. "Show me," I pleaded. "Give me a sign, please."

Don had planted a rosebush for me that summer that was supposed to bear yellow roses. He had always called me his "yellow rose of Texas." The plant had so far been disappointing as it had not produced one bud in three months. Now my gaze landed on that rosebush. Startled, not believing what I was seeing, I got up and went closer for a better look. One stem had many perfect buds on it, just opening. There were six perfect yellow buds, one for each year of our union. Tears welled in my eyes as I whispered a "thank you." A perfect yellow rosebud rested in Don's hands the next day at his funeral.

Patricia Forbes

One Last Good-Bye

I have sought to come near you,
I have called to you with all my heart; and
when I went out toward you
I found you coming toward me.

JUDAH HALEVI

The hospital room, hushed and dim, had come to seem somehow unreal to me as the day slowly passed, as though I were witnessing a tableau within a darkened theater. Yet the scene was sadly real—my brother, sister and myself, each lost in our own thoughts, silently looking on as our mother, sitting at our father's bedside and holding his hand, talked softly to him even though he was not conscious. Our father, after years of patiently with-standing the pain and indignities of a terminal illness, was near the end of his struggle, and had slipped quietly into a coma early that morning. We knew the hour of his death was at hand.

Mother stopped talking to Dad, and I noticed that she was looking at her wedding rings and smiling gently. I smiled, too, knowing that she was thinking of the ritual that had lasted for the forty years of their marriage. Mother, energetic and never still, was forever ending up with her engagement and wedding rings twisted and disarranged. Dad, always calm and orderly, would take her hand and gently and carefully straighten the rings until they were back in place. Although very sensitive and loving, the words "I love you" didn't come easily to him, so he expressed his feelings in many small ways, such as this, through the years.

After a long pause, Mother turned to us and said in a small sad voice, "I knew your father would be leaving us soon, but he slipped away so suddenly that I didn't have the chance to tell him good-bye, and that I love him one last time."

Bowing my head, I longed to pray for a miracle that would allow them to share their love one final time, but my heart was so full that the words wouldn't come.

Now, we knew we just had to wait. As the night wore on, one by one each of us had nodded off, and the room was silent. Suddenly, we were startled from sleep. Mother had begun to cry. Fearing the worst, we rose to our feet to comfort her in her sorrow. But to our surprise, we realized that her tears were tears of joy. For as we followed her gaze, we saw that she was still holding our father's hand, but that somehow, his other hand had moved slightly and was gently resting on Mother's.

Smiling through her tears, she explained:

"For just a moment, he looked right at me." She paused, looking back at her hand. "Then," she whispered in a voice choked with emotion, "he straightened my rings."

Father died an hour later. But God, in his infinite wisdom, had known what was in our heart before any of us could ask him for it. Our prayer was answered in a way that we all will cherish for the rest of our lives.

Mother had received her good-bye.

Karen Corkern Babb

Belonging

With the freeway ahead of us and home behind, the photographer and I left on a three-day newspaper assignment.

We were bound for the Columbia Gorge: where the Columbia River carves a mile-wide path between Washington and Oregon; where windsurfers come from across the country to dance across waves created by "nuclear winds;" where I would be far away from the world of nine-to-five, and deadlines, and routines, and errands, and rushing kids to baseball practices, and having to make sure my socks weren't left on the bedroom floor. Far away from the R word—"responsibility."

Frankly, it had not been the perfect farewell. Our family was running on empty. Our '81 car was showing signs of automotive Alzheimer's. We were all tired, cranky and trying to shake colds. My eight-year-old son tried to perk us up with his off-key version of a song from a Broadway musical. It didn't work.

I had been busy trying to get ready for the trip; my wife Sally had been busy fretting because my three days of freedom were going to cost her three days of extra responsibility.

"Daddy, are you coming to hear my class sing Thursday night?" Jason, my eight-year-old, asked amid the chaos of my departure. Had I been Bill Cosby, I would have gotten a funny expression on my face, said "Well, of course," and everyone would have lived happily ever after— or at least for a half an hour. But I didn't feel much like Bill Cosby that morning.

"No Jason, I'm going to be out of town," I said. "Sorry." Giving Sally a quick kiss, I was on my way.

Now, hours later, I was far away from family, free from the clutter, the runny noses, the demands on my time. Knowing little about each other, the photographer and I shared a bit about ourselves as we drove. Roughly my age—mid-thirties—he was married but had no children. He and his wife had seen too many situations where couples with children had found themselves strapped down, scurrying for babysitters and forced to give up spontaneous trips. He told me how he and his wife had recently taken a trip to the Gorge by themselves. My mind did a double take. *By themselves? What was that like?*

I vaguely remembered that kind of freedom. Taking off when the mood hit. No pleas for horseback rides about the time you're ready to crash for the night. No tornado-swept rooms. Besides having no children, the photographer had no six-month-old french fries on the floor of his car, no Superman action figure legs on his dashboard and no chocolate-smeared road maps in his glove box. Where had I gone wrong?

For the next couple of days, despite a threat of rain, we explored the Gorge—thousand-foot-walls of basalt rising on either side of the Columbia, fluorescent-clad sailboarders, like neon gnats, carving wakes in the water. If the land and water were intriguing, so were the windsurfers.

There were thousands of them, nearly all of them baby boomers, spending their days on the water, their nights on the town, their mornings in bed. Every fourth car had a board on top. License plates from all over the country dotted the streets.

Some of these "board-heads" were follow-the-wind free spirits who lived out of the back of vans; others were well-established yuppies who were here for a weekend or vacation. In the evenings, the river's hub town turned into Oregon's version of a California beach town: boomers eating, drinking, and being merry, lost in a world of frivolity and freedom.

For me, seeing this group was like discovering a lost, ancient tribe. *You mean, while I was busy trying to put on jammed bike chains, these people were jamming to the rock beat of dance clubs? While I was depositing paychecks to be spent on groceries and orthodontic bills and college funds, these people were deciding what color sailboards to buy? Where had I gone wrong?*

On our last night, the cloudy weather continued, which irked the photographer and mirrored the mood that had overcome me; we both needed sunshine, only for different reasons.

As I stared from the motel room at the river below, I felt a sort of emptiness, as if I didn't belong. Not here. Not home. Not anywhere. Just as the winds of the Gorge were whipping the river into whitecaps, so were the winds of freedom buffeting my beliefs. Faith. Marriage. Children. Work. I had anchored my life on such things, and yet now found myself slipping from that fixed position. *Had I made a mistake? Had I sold out to the rigors of responsibility? Someday, when I was older, would I suddenly face the bitter-cold reality of regret, wishing I had gone with the wind?*

I was getting ready for bed when I spotted it—a card in my suitcase, buried beneath some clothes. It was from Sally. The card featured cows—my wife's big on bovines—and simply stated, "I'll love you till the cows come home."

I stared at the card for minutes, and I repeated the words. I looked at the same handwriting that I'd seen on love letters in college, on a marriage certificate, on two birth certificates, on a will.

As I went to bed, there was no need to

call the front desk and ask for a wake-up call; I'd already gotten one. The card bore through my hardened heart, convicted my selfish conscience, refocused my blurry perspective. I knew exactly where I needed to be.

The next day, after a two-hour interview, six-hour drive and three-block sprint, I arrived at my son's school, anxious and out of breath. The singing program had started twenty minutes before; had I missed Jason's song? I rushed into the cafeteria. It was jammed. Almost frantically, I weaved my way through a crowd of parents clogging the entrance, to where I could finally get a glimpse of the kids on stage.

That's when I heard them: twenty-five first-grade voices trying desperately to hit notes that were five years away. My eyes searched this collage of kids, looking for Jason. Finally, I spotted him. Front row, as usual, squished between a couple of girls whose germs, judging by the look on his face, were crawling over him like picnic ants.

He was singing, all right, but with less enthusiasm than when he's been told to clean his room. Suddenly, his eyes shifted my way and his face lit up with the kind of smile a father only gets to see in a grade-school singing program when his eyes meet his child's. He had seen me, a moment that will forever stay frozen in my memory.

Later, through a sea of faces, I caught sight of Sally and our other son. After the program, amid a mass of parent-child humanity, the four of us rendezvoused, nearly oblivious to the commotion surrounding us.

I felt no emptiness, only connectedness. How could one man be so blessed?

In the days to come, I resumed my part in life as a bike-fixer and breadwinner, husband and father, roles that would cause a windsurfer to yawn.

But for all the excitement of riding the wind, I decided, I'll take the front-row smile of my eight-year-old son any day.

And for all the freedom of life in the Gorge, I'll take the responsibility of caring for the woman who vowed to love me till the cows come home.

Bob Welch

More Chicken Soup?

We enjoy hearing your reactions to the stories in *Chicken Soup for the Soul* books. Please let us know what your favorite stories were and how they affected you.

Many of the stories and poems you enjoy in *Chicken Soup for the Soul* books are submitted by readers like you who had read earlier *Chicken Soup for the Soul* selections.

We invite you to contribute a story to one of these future volumes.

Stories may be up to 1,200 words and must uplift or inspire. To obtain a copy of our submission guidelines and a listing of upcoming Chicken Soup books, please write, fax or check our Web sites.

Chicken Soup for the Soul
P.O. Box 30880
Santa Barbara, CA 93130
Fax: 805-563-2945
Web sites: *www.chickensoup.com*

Supporting Children and Families

In the spirit of fostering more love in the world, a portion of the proceeds from the original *Chicken Soup for the Couple's Soul* go to the following charities:

For more than a century the **Boys & Girls Clubs of America** have offered kids a place to go, guidance, recreation, and a range of educational programs.

Boys & Girls Clubs of America
1230 West Peachtree St.,
Atlanta, GA 30309-3447

Phone: 800-854-CLUB
Web site: *www.bga.org*

The **Children's Miracle Network** is an international nonprofit dedicated to raising funds for children's hospitals, to care for children regardless of their family's ability to pay.

Children's Miracle Network
4525 South 2300 East, ste. 202
Salt Lake City, UT 84117
Phone: 801-278-9800
Web site: *www.cmn.org*

837 Princess St., Ste. 302
Kingston, Ontario Canada K7L 1G8
Phone: 613-542-7240

The **PRASAD Project** is an international nonprofit organization dedicated to uplifting the quality of life for children and families living in poverty. In the U.S.,

PRASAD provides dental care and health education to children in need.

PRASAD
465 Brickman Road
Hurleyville, NY 12747
Phone: 914-434-0376

Who Is Jack Canfield?

Jack Canfield is one of America's leading experts in the development of human potential and personal effectiveness. He is both a dynamic, entertaining speaker and a highly sought-after trainer. Jack has a wonderful ability to inform and inspire audiences toward increased levels of self-esteem and peak performance.

In addition to the *Chicken Soup for the Soul* series, Jack has coauthored numerous books, including his most recent release, *The Success Principles, How to Get From Where You Are to Where You Want to Be* with Janet

Switzer, *The Aladdin Factor* with Mark Victor Hansen, *100 Ways to Build Self-Concept in the Classroom* with Harold C. Wells, *Heart at Work* with Jacqueline Miller and *The Power of Focus* with Les Hewitt and Mark Victor Hansen.

Jack is regularly seen on television shows such as *Good Morning America, 20/20* and *NBC Nightly News.* For further information about Jack's books, tapes and training programs, or to schedule him for a presentation, please contact:

Self-Esteem Seminars

P.O. Box 30880

Santa Barbara, CA 93130

Phone: 805-563-2935 • Fax: 805-563-2945

Web site: *www.chickensoup.com*

Who Is Mark Victor Hansen?

In the area of human potential, no one is better known and more respected than Mark Victor Hansen. For more than thirty years, Mark has focused solely on helping people from all walks of life reshape their personal vision of what's possible.

He is a sought-after keynote speaker, bestselling author and marketing maven. Mark is a prolific writer with many bestselling books such as *The One Minute Millionaire*, *The Power of Focus*, *The Aladdin Factor* and *Dare to Win*, in addition to the *Chicken Soup for the Soul* series.

Mark has appeared on *Oprah, CNN* and *The Today Show,* and has been featured in *Time, U.S. News & World Report, USA Today, New York Times* and *Entrepreneur* and countless radio and newspaper interviews.

As a passionate philanthropist and humanitarian, he has been the recipient of numerous awards that honor his entrepreneurial spirit, philanthropic heart and business acumen for his extraordinary life achievements, which stand as a powerful example that the free enterprise system still offers opportunity to all.

Mark Victor Hansen & Associates, Inc.

P.O. Box 7665

Newport Beach, CA 92658

Phone: 949-764-2640 • Fax: 949-722-6912

Web site: *www.markvictorhansen.com*

Who Is Barbara De Angelis, Ph.D.?

Barbara De Angelis, Ph.D., is interna-
tionally recognized as one of the foremost
experts on human relations and personal
growth. As a bestselling author, popular
television personality and sought-after
motivational speaker, she has reached mil-
lions of people worldwide with her positive messages about love, happiness and
the search for meaning in our lives.

Barbara is the author of nine bestselling
books which have sold over 4 million
copies and been published in twenty lan-
guages. She has hosted her own daily

television show for *CBS TV* and her own popular radio talk show in Los Angeles. Barbara's first television infomercial, *Making Love Work,* which she wrote and produced, won numerous awards and is the most successful relationship program of its kind.

For more information about Barbara's books and tapes, or to schedule her for a presentation, please contact her at:

Shakti Communications
12021 Wilshire Boulevard, Suite 607
Los Angeles, CA 90025
Phone: 800-682-LOVE
E-mail: *shakti97@aol.com*

Who Are Mark and
Chrissy Donnelly?

A husband and wife who exemplify the kind of loving couple these Chicken Soup stories portray, Mark and Chrissy Donnelly began their marriage with a decision to spend as much time together as possible—both in work and in spare time. Mark recounts how, during their honeymoon in Hawaii, they planned dozens of ways to leave their separate jobs and begin to work together on meaningful projects. Compiling a book of stories about loving couples was just one of the ideas.

Of the Couple's Soul project, Mark and Chrissy say they were drawn even closer together through the experience of meeting other loving couples and reading their stories. As a result, the Donnellys now strive to minimize their time apart and continue learning new ways to practice love and commitment in their daily lives.

Mark also serves as president of The Donnelly Marketing Group, expanding the Chicken Soup message to people around the world through special projects. Mark is former vice president of marketing for his family's successful building materials business. Chrissy was formerly a CPA with Price Waterhouse.

They live in Paradise Valley, Arizona. Mark and Chrissy can be reached at:

3104 E. Camelback Rd., Suite 531
Phoenix, AZ 85016
Phone: 602-604-4422 • Fax: 602-508-8912
E-mail: *soup4soul@home.com*

Contributors

If you would like to contact any of the contributors for information about their writing or would like to invite them to speak in your community, look for their contact information included in their biography.

Karen Corkern Babb lives in Baton Rouge, Louisiana, with her husband, Barry, and her five-year-old redhead, Collin Gabriel. She is the executive director of the Louisiana Association of Museums. Karen holds a bachelor of arts in art history from Louisiana State University and master of arts in museum science, with a concentration in administration, from Texas Tech University. She has held various museum positions during her career, but her most recent was at the West Baton Rouge Museum as its first professional director. The last five years have been eventful ones and have provided many learning experiences as her family has battled her husband's cancer. Their fight has been successful, and the story of her father's illness and her parents' last good-bye always reminds her to be grateful that their own last farewell was not yet meant to be.

Don Buehner is in business for himself and resides in Salt Lake City, Utah with his wife, Susan and their six-month-old son, Teancum. Don has an MBA from BYU. This story is dedicated to his daughter, Cesca Alice, 1994-1997. Don can be reached by e-mail at *donbuehner@ allwest.net* or 2584 N. SR 32, Marion, UT 84036, phone: 435-783-6734 or fax: 435-783-6736.

Thomas F. Crum's story was excerpted from *The Magic of Conflict* (Simon & Schuster). Crum offers training in conflict resolution as well as experiences in "The Magic of Skiing" in Aspen and "The Magic of Golf" in Tucson. Tom's second book *Journey to Center* (Simon & Schuster) offers humorous and insightful stories about getting centered. For more information you may reach Tom at Aiki Works, Inc., Box 251, Victor, NY 14564 or at *www.aikiworks.com*.

Jacklyn Lee Lindstrom is from the friendly town of Savage, Minnesota, and recently retired from the workforce rat race. She has at last been able to concentrate on her two loves—writing and painting. She has been published in Chicken Soup for the Mother's Soul and First for Women. She enjoys writing about the lighter side of family living because, as she says, after raising kids, horses and dogs, smiles last longer than tears and make better wrinkles. She can be contacted at 13533 Lynn Ave. S, Savage, MN 55378 or by calling 612-890-9333.

LeAnn Thieman is an author and nationally acclaimed speaker. A member of the National Speakers Association, LeAnn inspires audiences to truly live their priorities and balance their lives physically, mentally, and spiritually while making a difference in the world. She coauthored This Must Be My Brother, a book recounting her role in the daring rescue of three hundred babies during the Vietnam Orphan Airlift. To inquire about her books, tapes and presentations, contact her at 112 N. College, Fort Collins, CO 80524, phone: 800-877-THIE-MAN or online at *www.LeAnnThieman.com.*

David L. Weatherford, Ph.D., is a child psychologist and freelance writer. He writes poems, songs and essays about love, relationships, overcoming adversity and spiritual matters. He is currently working on his second book, in which he examines the role of suffering in life. While David draws on many sources for his varied writings, his romantic poems are inspired by his best friend and soul mate, Laura. You may reach David at 1658 Doubletree Lane, Nashville, TN 37217.

Bob Welch is features editor of *The Register-Guard* newspaper in Eugene, Oregon and author of *A Father for All Seasons* (Harvest House, $14.99). He has been published in *Reader's Digest, Sports Illustrated* and *Focus on the Family.* Bob may be reached at 409 Sunshine Acres Dr., Eugene, OR 97401 or e-mail him at *bwelch1@concentric.net.*